LAKE WAUBEEKA

LAKE WAUBEEKA

· A COMMUNITY HISTORY ·

JEFFREY S. GUROCK

THE
History
PRESS

Published by The History Press
Charleston, SC
www.historypress.com

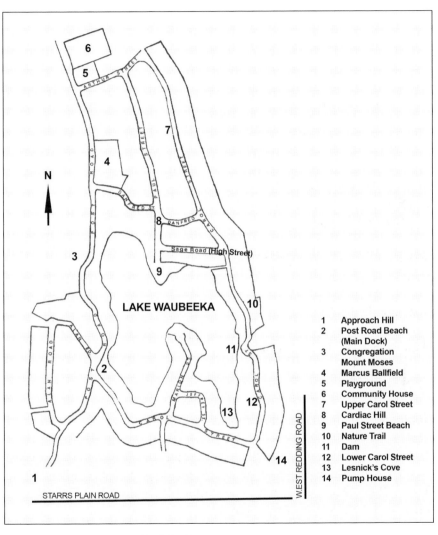

LAKE WAUBEEKA

1 Approach Hill
2 Post Road Beach
   (Main Dock)
3 Congregation
   Mount Moses
4 Marcus Ballfield
5 Playground
6 Community House
7 Upper Carol Street
8 Cardiac Hill
9 Paul Street Beach
10 Nature Trail
11 Dam
12 Lower Carol Street
13 Lesnick's Cove
14 Pump House

STARRS PLAIN ROAD

WEST REDDING ROAD

Map of Lake Waubeeka composed by Debra Burger.

CONTENTS

ACKNOWLEDGEMENTS

We are pleased to acknowledge Waubeekans, past and present, who love our lake community and have been a part of its history over seventy years:

Jonny Bellman family
Benitez family
Arthur Brody and Suanne Lowy McManus
Brown and Lantz family in memory of Milton Brown
Bruckman-Jureller and Colton-Goldfarb families in loving memory of our
    friend Michael Courtian
Debra and Frederick Burger
Richard Cantor and Esther Altmann
Gloria, Cubby, George, Adam and Doug Cohen
Victor and Carol Cohen
Courtian-Troy family
Diamond-Ross family
Edelstein family
Michelle Friedman and Benjamin Belfer family
Jennifer Holin Rubel Gitto
Goldberg family
Greenberg-Yager family
Greenstein-Koppelman family
Gurock family

Jules and Navah Harlow
Hastings family
Marc Jaffe, in memory of Harold and Frieda Jaffe
Judd family
Kessler family
Koenigsberg family
Bruce and Sharon Kutner
Dov and Nancy Lerea
Paul Levy family
Monnie Newman
Nellie, Louis, Abram, Nina and Aaron Orwasher
Stephen and Pauline Pearlman
Reitman family
Stuart Rosen and Judith Friedman Rosen
Rob and Sharon Sass
Schenker grandchildren in memory of Fannie and Barney Schenker
Sandy and Joan Schenker in memory of Fannie and Barney Schenker
Dan Schwartz family
Shwide-Donofrio family
Sinowitz family
Small and Schumann families
Lenny and Suzie Stein
Stiel, Wayne and Marcus families
Charlie, Anne, Wendy, Michael and Beth Stone
Meyer, Millie, Andrew and Barbara Stone
Milton, Lillian, Jesse, Molly and Sarah Uhrman and Paula Doerfel
Yehuda-Rothschild family
Dave and Chris Zwang family

INTRODUCTION

This book is proudly dedicated to Jackson Asher Gurock, a fourth-generation Waubeekan. He is named—as is common in Jewish tradition—for my father, firefighter Jack Gurock, a Waubeekan original, who with my mother, Lee, helped clear the roads and paved the way for the rise of a remarkable community. Jack was a long-term treasurer (1958–72) of the Lake Waubeeka Association (LWA), a supporter of Congregation Mount Moses and a pursuer of peace during some contentious early days of the synagogue's existence. But he is best remembered for playing a sterling second base or as a rock-ribbed catcher with an unlit cigar in his mouth in the men's softball league. So as much as Jackson carries within him Waubeeka genes, I possess a memory bank of personalities, events and some controversies that have sparked and sometimes roiled our community. These personal bona fides carry with them a challenge.

For as much as I am a trained professional historian who looks for objective documentation to narrate my stories, I am also a primary source for this volume. I have been on our mountain for seventy summers. So I have to be careful not to presume what I recall happened as fact and is not just one person's memory. In other words, I have dedicated myself, throughout this labor of love, to ascertain to what extent my "truth" is the truth. To address this dilemma, common to all who write contemporary history about places they believe they know so well, I have turned to the LWA's archive, much of which was lovingly developed by Harold B. Pollack, autodidact extraordinaire. The archive was especially useful in chapter 4 of this history, which documents some important board and community disagreements and decisions of the 1950s. Pollack also took some of the iconic early photos of life on the lake that adorn the Community House, some of which appear in this book. Complementing these core documents, we possess a detailed, personal history of the early years of the lake, *"It Couldn't Be Done" or the Story of Lake Waubeeka*, that its first president, Sidney Klein, composed. He was the driving force behind the rise of the community. We are grateful that his wife, Beverly Klein, granted us permission to use this document. Twice, in conjunction with our fortieth and fiftieth anniversaries, Waubeekans penned their memories. The fortieth anniversary brochure is titled *Lake Waubeeka: The First Forty Years*. The fiftieth anniversary document is called *Waubeekans Past and Present Share Their Fond Memories of Lake Waubeeka*.

In preparation of this book, I turned to my friends for their recollections of central issues in the community's history and have been gratified by their responses. Some of what they wrote to me has found its way into this history, usually set off by quotation marks. All the memoirs that were shared are now in the LWA's Archive. Nextdoor, a social network service, was also a resource for recent community discussions. Together, these sources constitute a time capsule that I hope a future historian will consult in writing the next chapters of our story. In developing and seeing this project to publication, I am thankful for the enthusiastic and helpful assistance of Steven Frankel, Lenny Stein and Dave Zwang. I am enormously grateful to Debra Burger, whose wonderful map of Waubeeka beautifies this volume.

Our journey of seventy years at the lake consists of six themes or chapters, opening, in the first five cases, with my narration confirmed and elaborated on by what Waubeekans of my generation and those who are both older and younger than me have remembered or now experience. We look at the vision and processes that led to the building of the community. The focus then recalls the lived lives of parents and youngsters—through athletics, informal neighborhood activities and formal creative and performing arts—when Waubeeka was a summer community. The work then considers the transformation of Waubeeka into a predominantly year-round settlement. The book then presents the voices of those who live full time or sojourn during the summer at the lake today as they offer some of their hopes, aspirations and expectations for the community's future. The work closes with a fitting postscript praising our neighbors for their reaction to Hurricane Isaias in August 2020. Their come-together behavior bespeaks so much about what Waubeeka continues to be all about. Scores of photos with captions that often utilized neighbors' words with credit lines to contributors, along with some important documents, add depth to each episode.

Readers are, however, gently forewarned. Though the writing generally has an upbeat lilt, a function of my affection for Waubeeka, we understand that our community has never been, and is not today, Shangri-La. Thus, appropriately on occasion, the story touches on controversies that have encumbered us. This aspect of Waubeeka's saga is carefully considered, most prominently in chapter 4. Some of the issues from back in the day have been resolved. Others have not or have repeated themselves.

I hope that I have gotten our history right. After all, even if what appears here engenders some disagreements about what transpired over seventy years among folks from Carol Street, around Post Road and within all the streets in between, I look forward to avoiding strident censure and to many more untrammeled summers on the Paul Street beach, with my ball cap on my head, reading a book, with a watchful eye on Jackson swimming inside the shallow water area and eventually making it out to the raft as he, and all children of Waubeeka, enjoy the bounties of our beloved community; a little piece of heaven off Route 7 in Danbury, Connecticut. Let us begin!

1

TEN DOLLARS DOWN

The Settling of Lake Waubeeka

The founding of Lake Waubeeka dates back to a meeting of the Ner Tormid Society (NTS) in the spring of 1950 close to a quarter century into the organization's existence. The name of the association was derived from the Hebrew term "Eternal Light," the light fixture that is mounted in front of the Holy Ark in synagogues. This fraternal organization of Jewish firefighters was founded in 1925, primarily to serve as a social welfare organization to help out sick members and to support the families of those who died on the job. But in time it also played an advocacy role for its minority group membership.

The interwar period was a time of ethnic identification and tensions within the Fire Department of New York City (FDNY), and Jews wanted a seat at the table next to—but perhaps not alongside—members of the German American Steuben Society, the Irish American Emerald Society, the Italian American Colombian Society and eventually the African American Vulcan Society.

As far as anti-Semitism was concerned, beginning in 1933, the persecution of Jews in Germany created hard feelings in the firehouses among those who either applauded or despised what Hitler was doing. But, on balance, there was considerably more tension between Hibernians and Hebrews due primarily to a seismic change in hiring policies that an Italian American mayor initiated. Under Mayor Fiorello LaGuardia, prospective civil servants were forced to qualify through a closely monitored, and highly competitive, exam system. Prior to that time, more

Memorial to the Ner Tormid Society. *Courtesy of Steven N. Frankel [SNF].*

often than not, teachers, police and firefighters, among others, got their posts through political connections. The Irish dominated the all-powerful Tammany Hall patronage machine. Now the Irish found themselves fighting against and losing out to Jews—who did well in these exams—for coveted Depression-era positions. By the end of World War II, the close to one thousand Jews who were on the job—most of them came aboard in the 1930s—constituted one-tenth of the FDNY's cohort.

After the war, as greater occupational opportunities opened up for Jews, relatively few of them entered the department. As the veterans aged out, this heroic sort of service proved to be a single generational phenomenon. The membership at the NTS declined, even if in 2020 it has been estimated that there were approximately three hundred Jews in the organization. But only a few of them are scions of the men of the 1920–50 membership. The numbers presently include men and women who work in the EMT division, those who serve in firehouses and Jewish civilians who hold desk jobs in FDNY offices. But while still in its heyday, the NTS turned to a very different concern: the health and welfare of the baby boomer boys and girls. These youngsters eventually became attorneys, bankers, actuaries, scientists, journalists, physicians and the like.

In the mid-1900s, more than ever, there was a desire to get youngsters out of the city and place them for a few weeks or months in bucolic settings away from the heat and grime. Swim and beach clubs on the perimeters of the five boroughs would not do, nor would sprinklers in Gotham's public parks. At night, they returned to hot, generally not air-cooled apartments. Making matters much worse, a polio epidemic hit the country, reaching its peak in 1952. To prevent the spread of the dreaded disease, the city closed public swimming pools. People even were admonished to not drink from water fountains and to avoid amusement parks.

It was in the spirit of those times of family concerns that, in 1947, the NTS created a Camp Committee with Sidney Klein as its chair. After surveying what other groups had been doing for their youngsters, he realized that, for a minimal outlay of funds, the NTS could do more than just build a camp. Its members could create a bungalow colony where children and their folks could sojourn together during the summer. Crucial to making his idea a reality was the availability of funds from the federal government. At that juncture, the Federal Housing Administration (FHA) was in the business of providing funds for "secondary housing," especially to the families of veterans who had performed so magnificently in the recently concluded World War II.

In due course, Klein shared his idea with his friend and fellow firefighter Barney Schenker, along with Julius Pine, Phil Wigler, Bob Green and Henry Kramer, who served with him in Bensonhurst's Engine Company 253. They shared his enthusiasm. It fit their families' needs, with their

Waubeeka project hatched
in a Brooklyn firehouse. *Lake
Waubeeka Archives [LWA]*.

preteen children fully in mind. Klein had a particularly talented little girl
at home—eight years old in 1950—who liked to sing and was blessed with
perfect pitch. Years later, his daughter would be known to the world as
Carole King.

On May 10, 1950, Klein and his associates presented the bungalow
colony idea at a special meeting of the NTS. What made this brotherhood
gathering unique was that the wives of Jewish firefighters were invited to
attend. Reportedly, one hundred attendees signed on to the plan through
an initial down payment of ten dollars with the understanding that their
initial investment would be refunded in full if the project failed. Before
the meeting adjourned, Klein was elected president of an organization,
Ner Tormid Inc., to move the idea forward. Work-in-progress committees
were constituted, consisting of fourteen men and one woman, Pearl Pine.
Family memories have it that NTS rank-and-file member Charley Rubel
came home from the meeting upbeat about his ten dollars down only to
find that his wife was less than enthusiastic about his action, which augured
to eventually cost them several thousand dollars if the project got off the
ground. But soon, his "winning rationale" was that the lake community
would get their two children out of the city during the polio epidemic.

Armed with a mandate from the NTS brothers and allied sisters, the search began to find a suitable locale for the project. Upstate New York and Connecticut newspapers carried NTS solicitations, and local agents were queried about available parcels in their regions. After a false start with a tract of land in Pawling, New York, an ad in the Danbury *News-Times* led a broker of "desirable farms and country homes" to proffer a 606-acre property that included a beautiful 36-acre lake. Locals knew the area as Lake Waubeeka, situated off Route 7, on a high elevation called Mount Moses. An "old-timers' theory" has it that Waubeeka is an indigenous name meaning "high water." The large expanse of land was basically virgin territory though Boy Scouts in the area used it for swimming, camping and fishing. There were four broken-down shacks on the premises. To reassure himself that he was not on a quixotic journey, Klein turned to, among others, his long-time friend Mac Pearlman, who was shown the territory and asked: "What do you think?" He replied: "Let's do it!" Pearlman family tradition has it that they were up on the mountain even before the steep, winding Approach Hill was constructed. At first, the way up was through a narrow pass from where the Pump House would eventually stand off West Redding Road.

After negotiations, the land was purchased for $90,000 ($75,000 in cash and a $15,000 mortgage). To seal the deal required the approval of two Danbury Town Boards—theoretically a significant barrier, as just down the road in Ridgefield and other tony towns, Jews were not wanted. But the newcomers had "local friends" like Rosie Blake, who owned land that abutted Waubeeka. With their neighbors' assent, it then remained for the founders to address the challenging tasks of finding "builders for the homes, contractors for roads and water, mortgage financing, FHA approval…and solutions to other problems."

In 1954, the community returned the favor to Danbury residents who welcomed them when "the firemen arranged to bring FDNY equipment

Real Estate Wanted

ASSOCIATION WANTS to Buy large tract, 350 to 1,000 acres, with large lake, within 100 miles of New York City, for development as bungalow colony. Give complete details in first letter to L. Zwicker, 515 East 14th Street, New York 9, New York.

Advertisement placed in the Danbury *News-Times*, November 17, 1950. *LWA*.

Sheet #10 – Lot No. List – Danbury, Conn.

Plot No.	Name	Order No.
283	Mac & Sylvia Perlman	1
284	David Block	4
285	Bernard & Minnie Block	3
286	Arthur C. & Lucille Klevins	18
287	Sam & Ida Turits	5
288	Jack & Belle Fried *Fred*	6
300	Milton Koerner	196
301	Martin Feyer	200
302	Saul Solomon	208
303	Jack Solomon	209
304	Abraham & Yetta Feldman	231
306	Irving Davidson	239
~~307~~ *305* / 307	Sol Epson – *change over to #305* / *S. Bernstein*	242
308	Julius Simon	243
60 ~~309~~	Herbert Friedman	241
310 / 324	Samuel I. Bernstein *change to #307* / *S. Coppersmith*	245
328	Abraham Rich	192
329	Herbert Mendelow	193
~~330~~ *330*	~~Sid Brody~~ *Ferken*	195
331	Leonard & Alice Mendelson	194
332	Kermit Hirsch	206
333	David Hirsch	205
334	Milton Held	207
335	David Held	211
336	Herman T. Robins	244

to help pump out the downtown" at a time when a tremendous flood from Hurricane Carol inundated the city. Occupying high ground, Waubeekans were spared some of the miseries of town folks even though their lake's dam overflowed. And then, in 1964, in the spirit that sometimes good deeds are rewarded, Danbury's Bravest and local Boy Scouts stood arm in arm

Opposite: Original list of deposits and lot assignments. *LWA*.

Left: A cabin at the Post Road Beach before construction began. *LWA*.

with Waubeekans in a successful all-night effort to put out a forest fire that threatened the lake and the entire wooded areas off Route 7 and beyond.

For all of their determination to build it—which brought them into contact, and sometimes conflict, with subcontractors of varying degrees of competence and honesty—there was the nagging fear that not enough families would buy into the project and share expenses. Among some of the ten-dollar down people, there were some who wanted their refund when they figured out the costs of construction and other collateral expenditures that ultimately made Waubeeka a substantial investment for civil service families. Several thousands of dollars were needed for a basic twenty-four-by-twenty-six shell of a bungalow—constructed by the Suffolk Development Corporation of Patchogue, New York—with its open ceilings, unfinished walls, sink, toilet, hot water heater, metal stall shower and a space heater that warmed one room, challenged homeowners to become handymen and handywomen. Often, the perplexed turned to their better-skilled neighbors for assistance.

When they were not fixing up their own places, there remained the chore of finishing common spaces. One of the most iconic early photos is of men and their boys and girls pitching in to clear the steep road—called Cardiac Hill—to the Paul Street beach. Then there was the problem that rain caused to the ballfield that turned it back into a swamp. The FHA had ruled this always-wet part of the mountain "unbuildable." Before bats and balls could be used, rakes and shovels were required to make the area playable.

This page: Interior of the basic bungalow. *LWA*.

Opposite: Clearing the road to the Paul Street Beach. *LWA*.

Most of the volunteer workers embraced these tasks as a "great community effort to improve the quality of life." But there were naysayers who questioned why Lake Waubeeka's initial board of directors—also volunteers and composed primarily of their own brother firemen—had left these jobs in the hot sun up to them. Even if they too might join in with their rakes and shovels, the most discontented felt that leaving such road and field work up to them was an arduous reminder that some of the promises that Klein, and those closest to him, had made in pitching the project had been slow to be fulfilled. It would not take long for this criticism to become public. It sparked the first debate over how Waubeekans managed their own community.

In the meantime, realizing almost from the start that the thirty-seven "Original Firemen" and their families on the mountain—whose names were enumerated in a document that Klein later composed—could achieve their endeavor, the association reached out to potential homeowners. They contacted their friends within firehouses, placed ads in civil service newspapers and initiated discussions with the New York Jewish fraternal organizations, most notably the Shomrim Society associated with the New

ORIGINAL FIREMEN AT LAKE WAUBEEKA
(as of August 1992)

Kenneth Aber
Nathan Aber **
Louis Auerbach **
Sydney Bennett **
Bernard Block
David Block **
Hyman Brown **
Morris Charnoff
George Danzig*
David Dicker*
Charles Dolgin **
William Drazen **
Louis Einbinder **
Martin Feuer **
Jack Fried*
Sam Friedlander **
Henry Gold **
Joseph Goodson*
Nathan Gruber
Jack Gurock*
Moe Haber **
William Heiberger
Ben Jacoby **
Larry Kay **
Harry Kessler
Sidney Klein
Arthur Klevins*
Charles Korn **
Henry Kramer*
Louis Krieger **
Samuel Levine **
Charles M. Levy **
Hy Litter **
Aaron Lurie **
Milton Manulis*
Albert Marks **
Rubin Maser*
Benjamin Nichamoff
William Pearl **
Max Pearlman
Julius Pine
Irving Rabinowitz*
Aaron Riff **
Julius Roll*
Sidney Rosenfeld
Irving Rothenberg
Charles Rubel*
Barney Schenker
Abraham Schifter*
David Schonzeit*
David Sherman

Bernard Shurin
David Sipkin **
Samuel Sirota **
Irvin Small
Isadore Steinbaum
Alex Steinman*
Charles Stone*
Harold Toback **
Milton Uhrman*
Bernard Weinberg
Philip Weinstein **
Philip Wigler
Harold Weisblut*
Lester Zwicker

* Deceased
** Withdrew - full refunds were
given to all who withdrew.

(If you know of anyone left
out, please contact me - SID
KLEIN 748-0561)

List of thirty-seven "Original Firemen." *LWA*.

24

York Police Department (NYPD), the United Federation of Teachers and the Jewish Postal Workers.

Harold Pollack, a forensic photographer for the NYPD—who took the photos of his neighbors at work and praised their "valiant" efforts—and his schoolteacher wife, Ruth, were among those attracted to the incipient community. Beyond these initiatives, the community picked up members through personal recruitment. Indeed, a tradition of chain migrations—one family telling those closest to them how grand life could be on the mountain—continued for generations. For example, in 1969–70, a group of thirteen families, friends from the Crescent Apartment complex in the Glendale section of Queens, came up together. Their "leader," who first introduced his neighbors to the place, was dubbed their "Moses who led them to the Promised Land."

More than a decade later, another chain migration brought some religiously observant Jews to the mountain, where they revitalized the existing synagogue. One of the members put out the word in New York's *Jewish Week* that the tenor at the lake was ideal for their type of Jewish lifestyle. She described her synagogue's community "as a model of interdenominational cooperation where we linger over kiddush and talk about ideas, art and politics." Saturday afternoons featured a discussion group on Jewish topics. She also intimated that some worshippers might unabashedly start "weekend *mornings* with yoga in the sand and the *days* continue with swimming," subtle, if significant, deviance from Orthodox Sabbath social behavior elsewhere. As of 2020, this congregational cohort consisted of some thirty to thirty-five families, constituting approximately one-eighth of Waubeeka's population.

When Waubeeka began, once a family, no matter whatever its background, opted in, the next crucial and exciting decision was to determine where the builders would construct their home. There was much open space from which to choose: approximately 75 one-quarter lakefront lots and 250 one-third acre "off-lake." A retrospective map and inventory of original homeowners—composed by Pollack in 1984—indicates that 244 families bought in in 1951 and an additional 20 a year later. Not all of the lots were ever improved. There also were hundreds of acres off the mountain that have remained undeveloped. Future generations of Waubeekans would debate what precisely might be done with this land.

Prime territory, understandably, was lakefront property around the peninsula. The Pine and Klein families wisely chose the most bucolic spots, while Schenker had his Carol Street house built facing the beautiful lake.

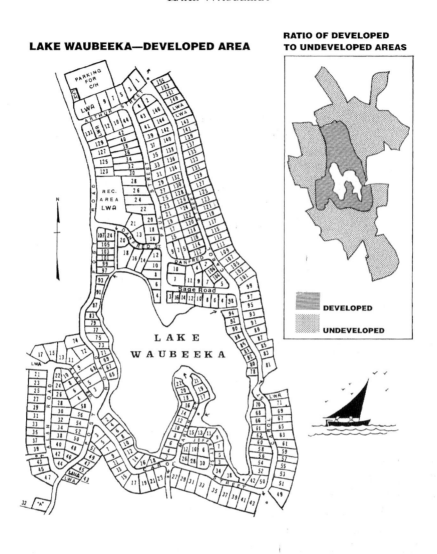

Map of developed and undeveloped Waubeeka lands. *LWA.*

Charley and Selma Rubel took note of where members of "the board picked their own lots and followed suit." Paul Street, on the other side of the mountain up Cardiac Hill and extending one-eighth of a mile to Arthur Street, had its own attractiveness, but for a very different reason. It would become home to families with young children who had yet to learn to swim. By 1952, Carol Klein, now of Jeffrey Street, was already ten years old.

26

Carol Klein as a
teenager. *SNF.*

Parents on the other side of the mountain feared that unsupervised
youngsters might drown. Some families with young children who opted for
houses on Alan Road, a steep walk up a winding road to finally get to the Post
Road Beach (aka the Main Dock), harbored similar apprehension. On Paul
Street, post office employee Meyer Stone and his wife, homemaker Millie,
for example, "were first given the opportunity to choose their lot" from a
map of the territory and "did not select a lot on the lake because their son
Andrew was only four" in 1951. They were afraid he might accidentally fall
into the lake. Desiring to reside next to their lifelong friends, fireman Irving
and his homemaker wife, Jeannette, who had a two-year-old son, Alan,
"selected two large adjoining properties on Paul Street." However, little did

Millie Stone paints her house. *Courtesy of Andrew Stone [AS].*

Andrew Stone waits for games to begin on Paul Street. *AS.*

they know that each of these lots had a twenty- to thirty-foot drop a short distance behind their future bungalow. On the other hand, when Andrew got older, he could see through the trees and also hear what was going on at the ballfield that abutted the steep drop. That common space was one of the areas where, beginning in 1958, community meetings were held, square and folk dances took place and an occasional classical music concert was offered and, of course, where land athletic activities were a daily feature.

2

SPORTS IN THE WATER
AND ON LAND

L ake Waubeeka's most outstanding athlete never played softball at the
  Pump House located off Starrs Plain Road, the first diamond for the
spirited games that were a fixture every Sunday morning almost from the
community's inception. Nor was he in the lineup later on when teams
battled on Marcus Ballfield at the junction of Danfred Street and Post Road.
(The athletic and early social venue was named in honor of Jack Marcus,
local entrepreneur and philanthropist, owner of Marcus Dairy, who helped
out the community in the 1950s and 1960s.) This solitary sportsman never
asked to be chosen when a basketball court was cemented at a corner of
the field. Tennis, paddle tennis and paddleball did not interest him. He also
rarely made an appearance at the beach. Swimming was not for him. To
the unknowing, he appeared to be anything but an athlete when he walked
around the lake with a strange gait. Only sports cognoscenti knew that
he was an Olympian; his sport of choice was race walking. A three-time
AAU champion before World War II who often wore the colors of the 92nd
Street YMHA, Fred Sharaga had represented the United States in the 1948
London games.

For most other people, the place to do their laps was in the two designated
swimming areas, while the most skilled "crawled" beach to beach or all
around the thirty-six-acre expanse. Presently, for safety's sake, most swimmers
attach a water balloon to a waist just in case they cramp up. Years ago, it was
required that a rowboat, with two qualified swimmers aboard, accompanied
those venturing outside the roped-off area.

The Pump House, site of the early softball games. *LWA*.

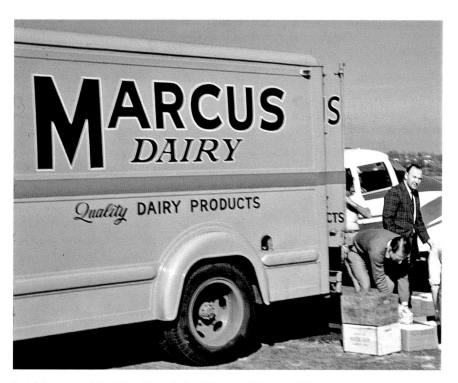

Jack Marcus readying his milk truck for delivery to Waubeeka. *Courtesy of Michael Marcus.*

Floating across the lake, 2020. *SNF.*

Maintaining what is Waubeeka's most essential natural resource has always been accorded the highest priority. No motorboats that might drip oil into the lake have ever been permitted. Algae levels are constantly and scientifically monitored. Beginning in 1998, "carp were introduced into the lake to remediate an invasive weed, Milfoil," which may annoy long-distance swimmers, "are still around but [are] not as prolific as in the past." Little fish find their way into the shallow water. Early in the summer of 2020, there was an unexpected visitor to the shore of the Paul Street beach. The appearance of a rather large snapping turtle excited kids and adults alike.

For most people, a dip in the lake or a long swim at their own leisurely pace has been a purely recreational activity. However, there was a time, from the 1950s to the early 1970s, when swimming turned decidedly competitive as the community applauded its water athletes of the year at its swim carnival. Although preliminary contests pitted boys against boys and girls against girls in age group races, the main event was the approximately one-fifth-of-a-mile race across the lake. In the early 1960s, those who would test their aquatic skills in front of a large crowd of parents and friends had a whole summer to prepare for their big moment. For two years, a varsity swim team—organized by lifeguard Noah Gurock—went up against clubs that represented neighboring towns and communities, starting with

Left: A snapping turtle visits Waubeeka, 2020. *AS.*

Below: Lake Waubeeka swim team. *LWA.*

Above: Roz Stein with her pupils. *Courtesy of Lois Greenberg Yager*.

Opposite, top: Boat race begins. *LWA*.

Opposite, bottom: The real action starts as boats are tipped over. *Courtesy of Gloria Cohen [GC]*.

Candlewood Lake and extending as far south as Wilton. And starting in the 1970s, lifeguard and water safety instructor Roz Stein taught a generation of youngsters how to swim in the cold early morning hours.

Stein was a strict "enforcer of the rules at the beach" during afternoon lake prime time. "If someone was playing rough in the water," she "would 'dock' them for a period of time or they had to go around the beach and pick up cigarette butts." When lifeguards ruled the swimming area seven days a week from 1:00 to 5:30 p.m., all sorts of rules governed water activities, most notably a prohibition against lifejackets or flotation devices. As a result, Stein's students—and those who learned swimming from other water safety instructors—could be proud when they made it to the rafts unaided. Not surprisingly, Stein's prized pupils were her own three sons, especially Adam, a frequent beach-to-beach champion.

Meanwhile, the other long-awaited event at that meet was the short but treacherous boat race around "the island," an outcropping of bushes and other wild greenery located directly across from the Main Dock. All went well and fair among the participants within this totally unsupervised happening

until the boats were hidden from the spectators' view. Then, battles royale began as boatmen and boatwomen fought one another, broke opponents' oars and tipped over boats. Only the strongest emerged untouched to garner their victors' medallions.

On land, from the 1950s through the late 1960s, the men's Sunday morning softball league was the prime-time sport. The competition was serious stuff—so much so that results of the games occasionally appeared

Charlie Stone at bat during batting practice at Marcus Ballfield. *Courtesy of Michael Stone [MS].*

in the *News-Times*. There were four long-standing teams: the Krafts, the Heilman-Reitmans, the Kesslers and the Goldberg-Gurocks. They were generally filled with relatives and friends—allegations about nepotism abounded—but the clubs also included some excellent players chosen in a preseason "draft." Every spring, the aunt of a legendary player compulsively called the league's commissioner to make sure her relative was included. She really had nothing to worry about. Her nephew was always picked in the first round. Such was the excitement that the league engendered. Some years, to further spice up interest in the lineups, teams were divided between "marrieds and unmarrieds" as grown sons and sons-in-law found their ways on to the lists.

Michael Stone shagging fly balls ready to be "chosen in." *MS.*

But it remained for 1967 to witness an imaginative tweak in the rosters that reflected the maturation of the next generation of Waubeekans. At that juncture, a large number of teenagers who chafed at being deemed "too young to compete" were allowed to have their own team. A Saturday Little League was not enough for them, even if they had sharpened their skills under the tutelage of volunteer managers who were among the best adult ballplayers. These quick and athletic boys embraced the competition, especially against their fathers. The "old men's" team, dubbed the A.K.s (*die alte kakes*, a Yiddish pejorative that need not be translated here), did not win a single game. But their sons proved their mettle and made it to the finals, only to lose the championship game to a squad of newly marrieds loaded with star players.

This page, top: Waubeekan youth softball league, 1970s. *GC.*

This page, bottom: Waubeekan paddleball teammates, 1980. *GC.*

Opposite, top: Waubeekan basketball team goes on the road to a New Jersey high school, 1976. *Author's collection.*

Opposite, bottom: Frog jumping competitors. *Courtesy of Mary Ellen Graziano [MEG].*

Building a playground, 1986. *LWA.*

Replica fire truck. *SNF.*

Lake Waubeeka Community Garden, established 2020. *SNF.*

Two years later, the men's league unraveled. The kids—now in their twenties—had become more interested in playing basketball, as round ball became the most popular land sport. Some of the old-timers returned to their athletic roots when a paddleball court was constructed. Meanwhile, in line with the growing national interest in tennis, this gentrified sport attracted its devotees while the next generation of Waubeekans started to play paddle tennis as their sport of choice. These boys, and now girls too, of the 1970s and early 1980s, also ran their own softball leagues. But their weekday competitions were just not the same as the contests between weekend warriors that had enthralled the entire community. Presently, net games attract almost all the players to the Marcus Ballfield. Runners and walkers use the jogging track that rings the neatly trimmed softball field. That diamond rarely witnesses a game. The paddleball wall is no more, replaced by a bocce court.

In the most recent decades, an amphibian event has entered the Waubeekan competitive sports calendar. Late in the summer, members of the youngest set take on one another in frog jumping contests. When these kids are not at the beach seeking their moment in the mud, coaching and coaxing their animal friends, they can be found doing climbing and hanging gymnastics at the playground built in 1986 a few steps down from the Community House. What makes this kids' space special—particularly for the grandparents who watch their youngsters at play—is its replica fire truck useful as a climbing toy. It is an appropriate reminder to all of Waubeeka's origins. In the summer of 2020, a community garden was created on Arthur Street; it is destined to be a bucolic addition to the future.

3

WHILE DADS WERE AWAY

For most second- and third-generation Waubeekans during the 1950s–70s, the happiest moments of their summers took place on Friday nights when their fathers returned to the mountain after their tiring week in the hot city. Though some dads were schoolteachers and had July and August respites and many firemen worked three days on, two days off or were able to schedule their vacations for a portion of the summer, so many were stuck in the metropolis either because FDNY men held second moonlight jobs or they worked nine to five, Monday through Friday. One memoirist has recalled how "on Friday nights (sometimes Thursday night) the cars would stream up the hill bringing weary dads who would delight their greeters with treats and comics from New York newspapers." Another remembered "waiting all week for Friday night to arrive" and his pop's "hugs and kisses." A third reminisced that "we would wait on the couch, stare [at] the window, awaiting for dad to pull into the driveway and we would all race down the steps to greet him." Not only did hugs and kisses follow, but also a quality home-cooked meal was in the offing. Some other fathers quickly scooped up their families and "went to Howard Johnsons for chicken or fish fries, a good way for the moms to have less cooking during the weekend." But they were sure to return by 8:00 p.m. for the weekly folk dances on the ballfield's basketball court and later at the Community House.

Come weekend mornings, many families would do their weekly marketing and on Sunday purchase the voluminous New York papers in Danbury or over the state line in Brewster, New York. Some families who were voracious

Above: Dad greets his children on Carol Street, circa 1960. *Courtesy of Arthur Brody.*

Opposite, top: Help on the monkey bars. *Courtesy of Amy Eisenberg.*

Opposite, bottom: A weekend family drive off the mountain. *Courtesy of Marcie Lowy-Wright.*

readers would use the availability of their automobiles on Saturdays to go downtown to Danbury's Public Library and pile up stacks of books for the week ahead. They were proud when the librarian told them "there was more action at the loaning desk" during the summer than other times during the year because of Waubeekan literary interests. For a significant portion of Paul Street, Saturday night was almost as important, when Manhattan bakery owner Louis Orwasher arrived with a full load of bread in his station wagon. While his wife, Nellie, distributed bread and rolls to her neighbors, Louis packed kids into three rows of seats; one faced backward. Off the happy gang went to Marcus Dairy for ice cream.

By contrast, for most youngsters, Sunday evening perhaps was the saddest moment in the week. For then, in one case, after a fine weekend of fishing and after "hugs and kisses from my dad, he got ready for his journey back to the Bronx." However, after the car pulled away, a twinkle in the eye may have replaced the tears. With his father away, the possibility for adult supervision had just been cut in half for the next five days.

Marcus Dairy Bar: A flavorful destination for Waubeekans. *SNF.*

While it was difficult for mothers to get off the mountain during the week, since most families had only one automobile, they were not isolated. Vendors serviced the community with some essential products. Community bylaws prohibited businesses. A nattily dressed driver, sporting a bow tie, bought up Duggan's baked goods. Marcus Dairy provided its loyal customers with its cold glass milk bottles. A greengrocer who drove a broken-down school bus sold fresh fruits and vegetables. The daily arrival of the Good Humor truck was, for moms and kids, a treat.

Telephone connections that multiple families shared, through a party line, linked them to the outside world. The phone could also be a source of local gossip if one listened in while a neighbor was on the line. By day, Scrabble was the game to be played on the beach. Most evenings, the women played mahjong and canasta on a rotating house-by-house basis. By day and by night, the moments between rounds were a good time to share the inside word on community goings-on. A newsletter was distributed with official announcements and reports about community events. As late as the 1980s, volunteer families typed up the notices, collated the pages and had a young Waubeekan distribute the information for a pittance. A few families had small black-and-white television sets available to anyone on their street who wanted to keep up on the news and shows even if their neighbors were away,

Paul Street dads, moms and kids on a Sunday afternoon, circa 1950s. *LWA.*

since doors were unlocked. And with their husbands away, and while their kids were out playing, there was time to wade through the multi-sectioned Sunday New York papers or to delve into the books borrowed from the public library.

But what about their often rambunctious youngsters? Most families had two or more children. Although a few preteen girls ran morning day camps for toddlers—basically a mothers' helper service—there was no money around the lake for a formal day camp with counselors, bunks and the like. To bring some structure, or perhaps control to the kids' lives, beginning in the early 1950s, a Women's Committee—complementary to the predominantly male Board of Directors—was established to plan activities on, and off, the mountain. The distribution of labor, one leader of the women recalled, was that the board looked closely at finances while their committee focused on entertainment activities for residents of all ages, but especially the kids, and tried to raise money to support their initiatives.

Neighbors from Post Road and Alan Road, Norma Brown and Jocelyn Zadoff, active women's committee members, recalled that "we women had lots of free time and not too much money, and therefore, the events we planned took ingenuity and lots of volunteers....We volunteers did many things that improved the quality of all of our lives."

THE WAUBEEKAN

| OCTOBER 1954 | HELEN GILNER, Editor |

GENERAL MEETING

During the month of October there will be a GENERAL MEETING for all Lake Tormid Shareholders. You will be notified of the Date and Place. Please make it your business to attend this meeting. This is the Annual Meeting for the election of members to the Board of Directors.

ROADS

Another portion of our roads has been completed. The new portion is Carol Street from Old Boston Post Road to the Peninsula and in and around the Peninsula which includes Marion and Jeffrey Streets.

These roads were completed with money borrowed from the residents of those streets. It is now the aim to do Old Boston Post Road, Danfred, Paul and Upper Carol Street in the same manner. Please lend your $100. to the Corporation and help finish the roads. This money will be applied against Lake Waubeeka Assessments to be levied in the future.

ALL RESIDENTS IN THIS AREA TAKE NOTE!

The Waubeekan, October 1954. *LWA.*

Before the Community House was built, homeowners hosted masquerade parties. Boys and girls were recruited for talent shows at the Post Road Beach. Plays that Genie Gingold, Carol Klein's mother, directed at the Community House involved scores of kids. In time, as some of the most talented grew up, they took over directing the performances. While for Brown, Zadoff and so many others, "the children [were] one of the main reasons the Women's Committee was formed," it also organized for themselves and for their spouses Yiddish culture programs, adult amateur nights, art shows, historical and current events discussions, Chinese cooking and self-help seminars, not to mention those weekly folk dances. Some men—those on vacation or the most energetic weekenders—joined casts of theatrical performances with Gingold leading them.

While many youngsters participated in these structured activities, what they liked most about their day-by-day summer lives was its informality, its spontaneity. A woman who grew up on Jeffrey Street recalled: "It was like being in camp without counselors….A typical day was going to the ballfield in the morning, home for lunch, rowing to the beach for the afternoon, home

Costume party on Paul Street, circa 1960. *Author's collection.*

This page and opposite top: Programs from Waubeekan Off Off Off Broadway shows. *Courtesy of Lori Diamond [LD]*.

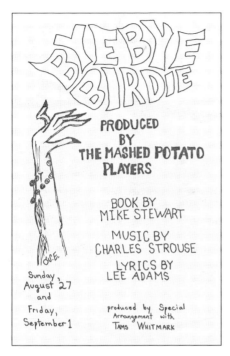

Scene from *Bye Bye Birdie* in the Community House. *GC.*

LAKE WAUBEEKA ** YIDDISH NIGHT

COMMUNITY SING

1. SIMAN TOV
Siman Tov Umazel Tov)
Mazel Tov M'siman tov) 3 X
Yeheh Lanu
Repeat above
Yeheh Lanu)
Ulecho Israel)4 X
[Repeat entire song.]

2. HAVA NAGILLA
Hava Nagilla, hava nagillah) 2
Hava nagillah, voh nis m'cha)
Hava n'ranana hava n'ranana)
Hava n'ranana voh nis m'cha) 2
U- ru u- ru achim
'Ru achim b'levsomeyoch (4 x)
'Ru achim 'ru achim
b'levsomeyoch.

3. HAVENU SHOLEM ALEICHEM
Havenu Sholem Aleichem (3)
Havenu Sholem Sholem,
Sholem Aleichem.

4. OIFN PRIPETCHIK
Oifn pripetchik brent a fayerl
Und in shtub iz heys
Und der rebbe lernt kleyne kinderloch
Dem alef - beiz
Gedenktzhe kinderloch, gedenktzhe
tayere,
Vos yihr lernt do.
Zagt zhe nach amol und takeh nach amol
Kometz alef- "O"

Az yihr vet kinderloch elter vern
Vet yihr alein farshteyn,
Vifil in di oisyes lign trern
Und vifil geveyn.

5. ROZHINKES MIT MANDLEN
In dem beys hamikdosh in a vinkl
cheder,
Zitst di almone, Bas Tsion, aleyn.
Yihr ben yochal ingele vigt zi keseyder
Und zingt im tsum shlofn a lidele sheyn.
A - a - a - a

Unter Yidele's vigele,
Shteyt a klar vays tsigele
Dos tsigele iz geforn handlen,
Dos vet zayn dayn baruf
Rozhinkes mit mandlen,
Shlof zhe Yidele, shlof.

6. TUM BALALAIKA
Shteyt a bocher und er tracht
Tracht und tracht a gantze nacht.
Vemen tsu nemen und nit farshemen,
Vemen tsu nemen und nit farshemen.

Tumbala tumbala tumbalalaika (2)
Tumbalalaika, shpil balalaika
Tumbalaika, freylech zol zayn.

Meydl, meydl, ch'vil ba dir fregn,
Vos ken voksn, voksn on regn?
Vos ken brenen und nit oyfern?
Vos ken benken, veynen on trern?

Narisher bocher, vos darfstu fregn?
A shteyn ken voksen, vaksn on regn.
Liebe ken brenen und nit oyfhern,
A harts ken benken, veynen on trern.

7. DI GREENE KUZINE
Tsu mir iz gekumen a kuzine
Sheyn vi gold iz zi geven di greene
Bekelech vi ro`te pomerantsn,
Fiselach vos betn zich tsum tantsn.
Nisht gegangen iz zi, nor geshprungen
Nisht geret hot zi, nor gesungen
Lebedik un freylach yede mineh
Ot azoy geven iz mayn kuzine.

Haynt az ich begegn mayn kuzine
Un ich freg ir: 's machstu epes, greene
Entvert zi mit a troyerdike mineh
"A za mazel oif Columbuses medineh!"

8. HINEY MATOV
Hiney matov uma nayim
Shevet achim gam yachad.

9. SHALOM CHAVERIM
Shalom chaverim, shalom chaverim,
Shalom, Shalom
L'hit ra-Ot, l'hit ra-Ot,
Shalom, Shalom

PAGE 1

This page: Yiddish Night at the Community House, song sheets in translation and musical accompaniment. *LWA.*

Beaver Pond, 2020. *SNF.*

for dinner, back to the ballfield in the evening to meet up with friends and maybe to someone's house to hang out." An off-the-mountain trek might take them down Starrs Plain Road to West Redding and its Emporium for penny candy and cheddar cheese pancakes two miles away. The adventurous would follow Post Road into the woods beyond the lake and end up at Marcus Dairy. On one occasion, hikers were fortunate enough to avoid the shotgun pellets of an angered farmer who saw them trespassing on his land. A safer trek within Waubeeka's undeveloped territory took walkers from a dirt road, a few steps up from the dam, to a beaver pond. In 1967, this territory became known formally as the Nature Trail. It has delighted not only kids who love flora and fauna but their parents too.

Boys on Paul Street would decide what to do each morning when they heard a ball bouncing on the street. Choose-up games would continue until "moms would call their sons for lunch by yelling their names or whistle their own unique whistles." Afternoons were reserved for the beach. Those not interested in land or water sports might go after turtles, frogs and salamanders or "skim rocks into the lake." And there was "the surrounding woods and unoccupied plots of land to be explored." For one young man, "the serenity of hiking the woodlands" was his "passion." This love of exploration in the wild would remain with him his entire life. Another fellow habitually stayed

This page and next two pages: Fun at the beach over many generations. *Courtesy of SNF, MEG and Josh Einstein.*

on his back porch recording music on his tape player. He was the street's disc jockey. He pursued that occupation when he grew up.

Although the loop around the perimeter around the lake was less than two and a half miles, boys and girls on either side frequently saw themselves as "partisans" in friendly competition with those who resided in another section of the community. Mark Swartz, whose family settled in the early 1950s and lived on Upper Carol Street, recalled that "my first opportunity to meet some of the kids from the *other* side of the lake came as a result of the punchball games that took place at the original Pump House ballfield." In time, there were so many fellows anxious to represent their piece of turf that the players challenged one another to all-star games. For Swartz, the "catalyst" that eventually "conjoined our group with many of the kids from the *other* side of the lake was not through our softball activities but rather the curiosity and desire of those *foreign* kids to check out the more popular Paul Street Beach" (emphasis his).

This territorialism continued for more than a generation. Adam Cohen has recalled that in the 1970s, "in the mornings, we might have played ball with kids from all over the mountain," and when they organized on their own their Little League, selections were not street by street. "We never seemed to hang out with the Post Road Beach (or Main Dock as some called it) crowd during the day. The Post Road Beach had 'them' and we were 'us'—at that time the differences seemed important." Nonetheless, shared experiences at the ballfield and at the beaches created lasting friendships among these young people that continued long into adulthood. In some cases, more than a half century after such bonding took place, those who remained close still referred to each other by their childhood nicknames.

In September 1961, the youngsters' own activities were formalized when, emulating what their fathers were doing on the board, and what the Women's Committee had done for them previously, a Young Waubeekans organization was established. Murray Kessler, who was known around the lake both as a Marcus Dairy truck driver and a fine softball player, was elected as its first president. Remarkably, at its outset, the new organization was given an important at-home lobbying assignment, as it was implored to "use their efforts to influence their parents in the making of their payments towards the building of the Lake Waubeeka Community House." Over time, the young people's association ran—under the leadership of its set of committees—an evening bowling league, among other weekly activities. Road trips took these teenagers to Stratford, Connecticut, for concerts and

Young Waubeekans' Car Wash. *LD*.

even a Shakespearean play, excursions that pleased their parents. Moms and dads were less than happy when their youngsters "mistakenly" bought tickets to the Candlewood Theatre in Brookfield for a performance of *This Is Burlesque* starring a "real-life stripper." Funds supporting both highbrow and decidedly lowbrow events were raised at a car wash and at a carnival that included a blackjack table with an underaged dealer.

4
DEMOCRACY AND DISAGREEMENTS

For those youngsters who were interested, the community also offered them lessons in participatory democracy. From the very start, in the spirit of New England Town Hall meetings, Waubeekans debated—often vociferously—both the mundane and transcendent issues of the day with a dog-eared copy of *Robert's Rules of Order* at hand. Though not all residents dutifully showed up—occasionally there were real problems with gaining a quorum (25 percent of members)—those who did often hung around until after midnight.

In their own circles, young people referred to these loudly contested evenings as the "Saturday night fights." As they watched the combatants, it was obvious that some of the men who argued "balls and strikes and outs" on the ballfield by day were at it again at night. Some parents were chagrined when they heard that rather than "go to the movies or bowling or to Marcus Dairy," their children preferred to watch their elders act out. They could hardly wait until the fun really began when the "good and welfare" agenda item came to the floor. At the same time, however, as these kids watched complaints ruled in and out of order, they acquired a rudimentary expertise in parliamentary procedures that would hold them in good stead when they matured.

The predicate for these budget, election and special meetings was the stipulation in the bylaws that homeowners had to approve the activities of the board, acting on their behalf from the prior meeting. Although the work of the board always was ultimately approved, difficult decisions often were made that engendered bad feelings that lasted a very long time.

Above and following eight pages: Lake Waubeeka Board leadership over the years. *LWA*.

Occasionally, neighbors used this public forum to complain about each other. These gripes were of little significance to the assembled even if, sometimes, old-timers attempted to pull rank over those who had moved in later. On one occasion, a woman whose family was on the mountain from the early 1950s told a fellow Waubeekan—a 1970s arrival—with whom she disagreed: "You Johnny-Come-Lately, who do you think you are, you were not here at the beginning?" But other times, hot-headedness was a function of dollars-and-cents concerns that roiled homeowners. Sadly, one time an overwrought dispute contributed to the death of a member who suffered a heart attack at the Community House.

In recent years, in addition to the meetings, Waubeekans had online venues to go after one another. The sometimes angry back and forth between neighbors on the Lake Waubeeka website and on Nextdoor caused one homeowner to suggest "that people can be a little [less] intense on community message boards." Though in the end, she mused that arguments were "actually a product of the passion and love that people have for the community."

BOARD OF DIRECTORS · 1979-1980
SHAPIRO, ZWICKER, POLLACK, LOWITT, SPECINER
BOYAR, GOLD, ROSENFELD, WIGLER, SINOWITZ, HANAUER

BOARD OF DIRECTORS - 1980 -1981
GOLDBERG, PEARLMAN, ZWICKER, LOWITT, SPECINER
SHAPIRO, GOLD, ROSENFELD, WIGLER, CHAYKIN, HANAUER

BOARD OF DIRECTORS - 1981 -1982
HANAUER, WIGLER, ROSENFELD, GOULD, PEARLMAN
GOLDBERG, SILVERMAN, EIFERMAN, DAVIS, LOWITT, WALDMAN

DIRECTORS 1982-1983

L.WIGLER, V.REITMAN, A.GOULD, J.GOLDBERG, P.EDELSTEIN, H.BLUM
J.DELIGDISH, S.DAVIS, B.SILVERMAN, I.EIFERMAN, E.PEARLMAN

BOARD OF DIRECTORS, 1983-1984

J.GOLDBERG, E.PEARLMAN, L.WIGLER, H.POLLACK, P.EDELSTEIN
I.EIFERMAN, D.WOLINSKY, B.SILVERMAN, S.RITTER, J.DELIGDISH

BOARD OF DIRECTORS, 1984-1985
J.GOLDBERG, G.BRUCKMAN, L.WIGLER, D.ZWANG
B.SILVERMAN, H.POLLACK, E.PEARLMAN, D.WOLINSKY, N.GILBERT

BOARD OF DIRECTORS, 1985-1986
J.GOLDBERG,* L.WIGLER, D.ZWANG, G.BRUCKMAN, H.POLLACK
D.WOLINSKY, N.GILBERT, B.SILVERMAN, E.PEARLMAN, J.DELIGDISH
* P.COUCHEVITZ, SUPT.

BOARD OF DIRECTORS, 1986-1987
WEINBERG, EDELSTEIN, GOLDBERG, KRATE, BRUCKMAN, POLLACK
WOLINSKY, SILVERMAN, GILBERT, DELIGDISH, ZWANG

BOARD OF DIRECTORS, 1988-1989
POWELL, KRATE, POLLACK, DELIGDISH, GOLDBERG
ZWANG, PEARLMAN, WOLINSKY, GILBERT, WEINBERG

BOARD OF DIRECTORS, 1989-1990
N. GILBERT, H. KRATE, E. PEARLMAN, J. GOLDBERG, D. ZWANG
J. POWELL, B. WEINBERG, P. BUCHOLT, D. WOLINSKY, J. DELIGDISH, H. POLLACK

BOARD OF DIRECTORS 1990-1991   6/9/91
H. BOROWIEC, B. WEINBERG, J. DELIGDISH, G. BRUCKMAN, E. KIRCHE
P. BUCHOLT, E. PEARLMAN, H. KRATE, H. POLLACK, J. GOLDBERG

G.ADAMS, P.DUBREUILH, M.CREIGHTON, G.McGEOUGH, B.KUTNER,
B.ZORN, B.WEINBERG, H.KRATE, P.APGAR, H.POLLACK

1997

67

Election Night at the
Community House.
LWA.

One frequently voiced complaint over the years was that employees' salaries were too high, even though the community had long been blessed with devoted caretakers, most notably Pete Couchevitz, who, starting in 1965 and continuing for more than a quarter century, kept the roads and water system in formidable shape. Pete also knew how to work the crowd of his admirers. Every summer evening, after a hard day's work, he and his wife, Lil, would drive slowly around the community in their truck, waving greetings to residents young and old. Pete kept an eye on youngsters' behavior—he knew them all by name—and quietly yet effectively reported any misdeeds to their parents. Thirty years after Pete's retirement, the question of how many people are needed to maintain Waubeeka's infrastructure was still debated both within the board and at general membership meetings.

Truth be told, the rank and file of homeowners was never a particularly trusting and docile bunch. As previously noted, and as a prime early example, although Sidney Klein was widely credited with making his dream of Waubeeka a reality, it did not take long for complaints to be raised about his management style and the performance of some original board members—who were his closest associates—in moving the project forward. In 1954, just three years into the community's existence, critics complained that the roads had not been fully paved either as a "private system" or linked up with those of the town of Danbury, that beaches had not been finished and neither had a "community house and other recreational facilities" been completed. Almost from the moment Waubeekans ascended Mount Moses,

Pete Couchevitz, Lake Waubeeka's beloved caretaker. *LWA*.

they dreamed and planned for the building of a social and cultural center. And there were allegations espoused of "irregularities" in "the type of audit made, the accuracy of the figures and the validity of results"—effectively an accusation of padded expense accounts. For Klein, "rumor mongering" and a hateful "whispering" campaign challenged his performance.

Stung by these attacks, in June 1954, Klein resigned from the organization's presidency. In a sharply worded four-page letter—complemented by a two-page addendum—he shot back, asserting that

> in my zeal, I have neglected my family, my job and my income....I have made it a firm practice to accept gratuities from no one and that includes the membership and...people we have done business with....We have had enough real problems to have killed this project a long time ago if not for the unstinting hard work and devotion of less men than you can count on one hand. AND NONE OF THESE CONSTANT BACK-BITERS WERE AMONG THEM. A little clique...has become a malignant tumor. [All caps his]

But, at that point, Klein said, he was personally unable to lead a counteroffensive.

However, Klein's step back did not last long. In November 1954, he wrote to the community that since the board, now headed by Marvin Kirsh, had failed in its "work...the past few months...I must again offer my services." To aid him in regaining leadership, he tendered a slate of ten other "men who have expressed their willingness to run with me." Soon thereafter, his campaign took a decidedly personal tone, as Klein, and his close friend Julius Pine, attacked, by name, members of the board who either did not attend meetings and/or were "delinquent" in meeting their own financial "obligations until extreme pressure was brought to bear." In a subsequent open letter, Klein and Pine asked rhetorically: "WHY does a certain member who has never had anything constructive to offer suddenly have ALL the answers ONLY IF HE and his slate is elected?" (Caps theirs)

In response, Kirsh, promoting his own "group of civic minded people with community spirit," argued that "we all know that a new look is really necessary" for a "constructive program aimed at achieving the most advantageous possible solutions to our problems....To do all...we must have Directors who will pitch in and do the work sincerely and honorably."

The contested election of December 1954 ended with a split decision. Notwithstanding the vitriol of the campaign, for a few moments, compromise was in the air. The rank and file chose candidates from both slates to serve on the board. And then those who were elected chose Klein as president and Kirsh as first vice president. Still, Klein's "victory" was short-lived. The subsequent election witnessed Pine voted off the board. This "disgraceful" decision, as Klein called it, convinced him to "resign from the newly elected board in protest."

In the years to come, in Klein's opinion, "those who had done nothing or very little when we really needed help took over and I know that although I was later elected to many boards, this little group saw to it that each new Board did not elect me as president."

What is certain is that for the next decade Marvin Kirsh served as Lake Waubeeka's president, and a core of board members were reelected time and again. No allegations of malfeasance were tendered against this group, and the long-hoped-for Community House was built in 1963. But some people griped quietly that the caretaker was more attuned to the needs of board leaders than to the rank and file. By the summer of 1971, there was a feeling around the lake that an oligarchy—even a generally benevolent governing clique—was just not right for Waubeeka. The core of the board had stayed in power through the practical politics of collecting proxies from those who did not attend the election meeting.

In August 1971, the community bylaws were changed, imposing term limits. From that point on, after a three-year term had expired, an incumbent had to wait two years before standing for reelection. (The protocols of term limits would be modified over the years, but the precedent had been set.) With this modification, it was hoped new blood with "fresh ideas" would course through Waubeeka.

However, once the "old guard" was weakened, the new boards found that few homeowners—starting with those who "sat on the beach and complained"—were anxious to assume often-thankless jobs. And there were those who liked the prestige of being elected but were inactive except when it came to in-camera discussions. In an attempt to weed out "do-nothings," one Waubeeka president tried to recruit—prior to their election—members who would assume "a portfolio," agreeing to head up a functioning committee. Interestingly, back in the 1950s, Sidney Klein had faced a comparable problem. He recalled, "With each regularly elected Board of Directors committees for various duties and functions were appointed. With very few exceptions, these committees and their members failed to perform their assigned duties, which then fell to me by sheer default." This dilemma would be a continuing problem for all subsequent administrations. Successive presidents would complain privately that "while there were eleven men and women on the board only six could be counted upon."

Meanwhile another issue arose in the mid-1950s and extended to the early 1960s that would have even more enduring implications. It would define what sort of community Waubeeka would be. The contretemps revolved around the question of whether the association would assist—even minimally—the construction of a synagogue on Mount Moses. Or, alternatively, should Waubeeka officially undermine, most definitively, the existence of a congregation in its midst? This battle was a veritable Jew versus Jew fight since the era of religious diversity on the mountain would not begin until the 1970s. Until that time, almost all homeowners were Jewish, though from 1964 to 1968, Peter Dotti, a Christian, was president of the association. It was in that era that some residents yelled at and remonstrated against one another about community identities and priorities. For a while, the majority of homeowners put themselves on the record as opposed to an established religious presence. Within this imbroglio, Barney Schenker, one of the founding parents of Waubeeka, was the central figure in this battle and the target of much criticism.

Announcing the building of Congregation Mount Moses's synagogue. *Courtesy of Gail Reiser.*

Indeed, Sid Klein's history, in offering a basic story line for this dispute, called it the "Schenker Affair." In 1956, when Schenker and his neighbor Michael Rosenbaum petitioned the community for a "hook up to the water system" for a modest synagogue building to be situated outside of community property, they were turned down. Prior to that time, the few who were interested in Sabbath services had met on a rotating basis at one another's homes. Once Rosh Hashanah came around Labor Day a tent was rented and pitched in a backyard of a home on Post Road for a larger crowd of worshippers. But now, as Klein told it, with permanence in the offing, there were "those who feared that the synagogue would 'compete' with a proposed Community House."

It is unclear from his reportage precisely how the congregation might *compete* against the community. But it is reasonable to presume that the always financially strapped organization worried that voluntary contributors to the rise of the house of worship would vote down a capital expenditure for the long-desired Community House. In this view, if money had to be spent on "Jewishness," it had best be earmarked in the social and cultural center for perhaps some secular Jewish program offering, like a

73

This page: Community House under construction. *LWA*.

Yiddish night. A significant number of these second- and third-generation Jews had that beloved ancestral language, with its songs and folk tales, in their backgrounds.

Or to put it another way, those who vocally opposed the synagogue were not all "self-hating Jews," as their opponents alleged. For example, one of the children of a board member who voted against the Congregation Mount Moses's (CMM) application pointed out that her "parents were active in the Anti-Defamation League of the B'nai B'rith"—an organization that fought anti-Semitism—and, earlier on in their lives, as "liberal, socially-progressive Jews, had supported rent strikes in the Bronx and backed Democratic candidates." Such activism back then was deemed another Jewish value, as was their sustained interest in Jewish cultural activities, especially programs in their parents' language of Yiddish. But a synagogue that created an enduring religious tenor that they had moved away from in their lives was not for Waubeeka. Beyond these thoughtful dissenters there were those on the mountain who wanted neither a Community House nor a shul. Both were expensive structures. The dollars-and-cents issue was always on their minds. Just a few years later, members of the Young Waubeekans would be asked to lobby their parents to pay what they owed expeditiously for the Community House project.

But archival documents hint of additional motivations among those who were strongly opposed to the synagogue. In the spring and then the summer of 1956, two "additional special meetings" were held to "consider and act upon the request by Congregation Mount Moses for the furnishing of water" solely for worshippers' bathroom use. The terse board minutes did indicate "Lake Waubeeka's articles of incorporation provide that water may be made available outside of the community if approval was forthcoming by the association." After a discussion, the issue was tabled until "attendance would be sufficient to vote on the proposal." Meanwhile, a board committee was empaneled to study the request and to report back to the membership.

On August 11, 1956, the committee rendered the results of its study. The text of the findings is not extant, but the minutes state that the recommendation was that "water service be granted providing there is nothing but religious functions carried on." Evidently, there were concerns that the synagogue group was out for bigger game and might create larger religious atmospherics at the lake. Such certainly was the viewpoint of the prime leader of the opposition, who was the chair of the committee, suggestive that the pro-shul position did not exactly receive a fair hearing. In any event, when the report was put to a vote, homeowners, by a count of 70–34, declined to affirm the motion for granting water to the congregation.

To be sure, most of those who voted "no" did not strongly oppose the idea of a shul. Most likely they felt that Waubeeka could not afford both a Community House and a congregation. A compromise idea that one building could house both would not fly. Could the synagogue people have their Friday night services in a designated room while folk dancing—even Israeli dancing—went on in the heart of the center?

Over the next six years (1956–62), representatives of the CMM tendered frequent appeals to the board to reconsider its stance. The petitioners' requests were routinely tabled. Finally, in August 1962, in a spirit of coexistence, the board approved the request for water and sent the application to the entire community for ratification. One of the prior, vocal opponents of the synagogue within the board now opined that "a spirit of trust between the congregation and the community was all important." However, the long-term leader of the anti-CMM group was unmoved. He not only abstained from voting at the board meeting but, in the days before the show-down membership meeting, also sent an open letter to fellow Waubeekans listing some twelve questions that congregational leaders had to answer to "avoid misunderstanding and confusion." Through this letter his consistent position of opposition to a Jewish religious presence—which most likely also informed his 1956 committee report—was made abundantly clear.

The interrogatories included:

- What exactly is meant by the term "religious services?"
- Are celebrations, parties, meals etc. held in conjunction with weddings etc. also be considered as "religious services?"
- What social and fundraising activities would be held in and on the organization's property?
- Will religious services, social and fundraising activities be limited only to members of the Lake Waubeeka community?
- Will any residences or commercial buildings be erected?

At a board meeting in February 1962, an unidentified board member—who clearly shared this negative point of view—wondered out loud whether CMM would hold bingo nights to raise funds, a common déclassé feature of synagogue and church life in the 1950s and even later. And perhaps, most critically: would the officers, members and supporters of the organization give full support for construction of a Community House? For the letter writer, "as a gesture of good faith," he asked, "Will CMM agree to wait for water service until water service is given to a Community House erected by the membership of Lake Waubeeka?" This disingenuous suggestion would have delayed CMM's modest plans indefinitely.

On August 15, 1962, at a special membership meeting that was quite contentious, the majority ruled by a *secret* ballot vote of 120 in favor and 30 opposed that the association would grant CMM water with the understanding that as "one community" they would all work together to build the long-awaited Community House and pay whatever costs accrued. However, a minority remained adamantly opposed to a congregation. Another long-term opponent went so far as to threaten that if the synagogue was at all connected to the community that he "would write to Hartford"—to the state capital—letting the secretary of state of Connecticut know that Waubeeka was a religious and not a nonsectarian institution. It is not clear what sort of legal relief he hoped to achieve. But his very suggestion angered at least one member, who rose from her seat and declared, "How would it look that Jews were against one another?"

The sanctuary of Congregation Mount Moses. *SNF.*

From that point on, Congregation Mount Moses would have the basics for a building—years later a social hall would be added—though a minority of their neighbors expressed their unhappiness in quite nasty terms. Some of the homeowners who lived close to the shul chafed at the lights and sounds emanating from across the street during prayers. In angry response, they "blasted their radios during evening Rosh Hashanah services."

Lake Waubeeka's thumbs up, after its turn down, did little to mollify Barney Schenker, who vowed to never set foot in the Community House. When property owners were assessed to support construction of the social and cultural center, he deducted what he deemed the pro-rata charge for the building. In response, the board placed a lien on his property. Eventually, Schenker paid his fair share but balked at paying a paltry "$77 charge involving the lien." That was the beginning of a dispute over whether he, and some others who aligned themselves with him, were obliged to pay for a variety of activities and community institutions that they determined were not for them. As the dispute dragged on—costing the litigants thousands of dollars—the battle became increasingly personal, as a few of his major opponents lived only a stone's throw away. Subsequent board leaders attempted to mediate the issues, but to no avail. The Schenker Affair wound through a tortuous journey within Connecticut civil courts, where the dispute lasted—in varying forms—for more than a generation.

By the time a new synagogue group began arriving on the mountain, only a few old-timers and their children even remembered that the battle had taken place. All that most Waubeekans knew or cared about observant Jews was that these newcomers paid their dues and a few of them served on the board. As far as their specific religious needs were concerned, there were no objections voiced when the beach parties were scheduled for Sunday rather than Saturday afternoon. There, the kosher hot dog and burger stand was placed next to the nonkosher table. Beginning in 2014, all Waubeekans who liked to dance the way that they had in the 1950s–1960s did not complain that the "sock hop" held in the Community House did not start fully until the Sabbath ended, when the observant Jewish DJ, who helped organize the event, spun his first platter.

However, in August 2019, a brief kerfuffle took place that, for a few unhappy days, suggested that there were limits to the larger community's willingness to accommodate this religious minority while questioning how neighborly some of the shul people wanted to be. The precipitant for this disagreement was the community's plan to show a documentary movie about the famous Woodstock concert under the stars at the Paul Street Beach, while across

This page: Sock hop in the Community House. *Top courtesy of Noah Gurock; bottom courtesy of John Tench [JT].*

the lake, some shul members were solemnly observing the start of a fast day. When "a holiday observant person" or "persons" alerted the projectionist about "the noise concern," he agreed—without turning to the board for its approval—to "relocate to the Community House." However, this decision did not sit well with a neighbor, who asserted that "one's religious beliefs… should not be imposed on the entire community. I did not sign any papers when I bought up here stating anything like this." She then sent out an email to "everyone in the community" whose address she possessed asking that if you "agree would you please forward it" to the board.

Not long thereafter, the board determined to keep the event at the beach. President Arthur Brody explained the decision in a letter to the entire community. He noted that he had received "a number of calls and emails… expressing dissatisfaction [with] moving the venue to the Community House." The majority's preference was for the beach, "where Waubeekans can sit underneath the stars and enjoy the great music with friends and neighbors." Having said that, he prayed that as Waubeeka "continues to evolve into a very diverse community that support many different cultures and beliefs…that we continue to respect and support our diversity."

The synagogue group proved to be of several minds in response to this decision. Its majority accepted the board's determination even as they expected that the Jewish calendar should be consulted in the future, as it generally did in the past. One voice that surely wanted an end to this

Waubeekans "chowing down" together at a beach party. *JT.*

80

disagreement declared: "We must be respectful of all Waubeekans just as they always strive to be respectful of us. I'm sure you all have noticed there is a kosher table at community events. That's quite something! We are one community. We must maintain this wonderful feeling of unity." However, a minority intuited from this incident that there was an undercurrent of unhappiness with them, a prejudice that had to be confronted. A spokesperson suggested that "personal, private, person-to-person approaches reinforce a clear implication and, in some cases, an actual feeing that we need...to be quiet, private and without attention because we really aren't entitled to the accommodation and/or the community will be outraged....We are entitled and I for one don't care who knows it."

5

FROM SUMMER COLONY TO YEAR-ROUND NEIGHBORHOOD

The bungalows built in the 1950s were for summer use only. A small space heater that warmed a portion of the living room was the only built-in source of warmth. It was useful, to some extent, on an unusually chilly July morning or late in August with the arrival of an early fall in Connecticut. But getting the mechanism to work was a struggle. A long, slim iron pole with a hole on the end, designed to hold a lit match, had to be extended down under the house to ignite the burner. On July 4, 1961, Sam Kraft was not careful when he let a few matches that he believed were extinguished fall among the leaves under his place. In seconds, the wood house was on fire, and in minutes, it burned to the ground. By the time the Miry Brook Fire Department truck arrived on the scene from its station off Route 7, there was nothing to do but to water down the adjoining houses and trees to prevent a further conflagration that threatened to engulf the entire street. As these volunteers did their cleanup and preventive work, FDNY veterans—ranging from firemen to a battalion chief—gave them much "advice."

Miriam and Rube Ozeck and their children Rita and Floyd were among a handful of Waubeekans who, early on, winterized their homes for year-round use. The story line of their first summers at the lake—from the early 1950s—resembled that of most of the original families. Rube's friend Julius Pine recruited Rube. The Ozecks chose a lot far away from the lake since Miriam did not swim. They did not "lock doors, never took the keys out of the car and the neighbors were more family than friends."

Miry Brook Fire Department ready to assist Waubeeka. *SNF.*

Rube, then owning a small trucking business, came home on weekends and on Saturdays was a vocal worshipper at CMM. However, in 1959, the Ozecks became exceptional Waubeekans. But some of the issues they faced—albeit in their case in acute fashion—would concern all twelve-month residents to this very day as Waubeeka moved away from its origins as a summer colony.

With Rube's business foundering due to onerous interstate commerce regulations, he returned for employment "to his roots… as a produce manager at the Food Fair in Canarsie." When, soon thereafter, he learned that a comparable job was available in a new Danbury branch of the supermarket chain, the family actually "voted" at a sit down at their kitchen table to move. Rube lived alone their first winter on the mountain and worked at night and on weekends "to winterize and expand the house for…year-round use."

After Floyd's Bar Mitzvah and the close of the school year in 1960, the family left the Bayview Projects in Canarsie for full-time residence in Waubeeka. For Floyd, the social and educational "reality" of what they had done only "kicked in once Labor Day rolled around and everyone went back to the city." His summer friends were gone. He "had to change schools, try to make new friends," and since Miriam did not drive, she was not available to pick him up if he wanted to stick around for after school activities. Such clubs, choirs and sports teams would have been a great way to make friends. Even the logistics of meeting the school bus was a challenge. With his dad already at work, he had to walk alone down and back from Carol Street to Starrs Plain Road since the Danbury Board of Education would not permit its buses to trek up the Approach Hill. Subsequent generations of year-round Waubeeka families would have to deal with that reasonable school policy. For Floyd, the move was a "difficult transition" and a "lonesome" one. The situation improved somewhat in 1963, when his older sister purchased a car and he earned his driver's license. Still, "by this time kids from school had their friends and activities all set and it became difficult to get involved with them." Need it be noted that there were no community activities to participate in the winter. The Community House was still an unrealized dream. Floyd impatiently awaited the arrival of his summertime friends starting around Memorial Day.

Harriet and Herb Krate, another of the inaugural year-round families, led a happier life on and off the deserted mountain during wintertime. In the summer of 1965, Harriet, the quintessential second-generation Waubeekan—she is the daughter of Fannie and Barney Schenker—moved with her husband into a newly constructed and well-heated home on Alan Road. Teenager Floyd Ozeck's daily logistical dilemma of how to get to school was not yet an issue for the Krates. Their eldest daughter, Jodi, was a toddler, and Susan was an infant their first winter at the lake. Their son, Seth, would arrive in 1969. By the time these youngsters were ready for kindergarten, Harriet had a driver's license and was able to taxi them daily down and back up from the bus stop. Come high school, the children were on their own. As important, with a second family car at her disposal, Harriet was able to frequent meetings of Hadassah—the Zionist women's social and philanthropic organization—and, along with Herb, attend the United Jewish Center, the long-standing synagogue in town. Jewish and Gentile friends within the city were their social circle since "there was nothing to do on the mountain."

The uniqueness and some of the problematics of these families' situation did not change much in the 1970s when Rose and Henry Schwartz and their children and the young marrieds Chris and Dave Zwang decided to live full time at Waubeeka. Henry, an electronics repair expert who opened a shop in downtown Danbury in 1973, avoided the burden of a daily commute to New York City. Herb Krate commuted daily to his job as a salesman an hour or so away in the Bronx. Henry Schwartz and stay-at-home mom Rose (later she would become a nurse) now lived but fifteen minutes away from his work. Their son, Dan, remembers initially being somewhat disoriented "by the quiet at night" when they were, after Labor Day, one of two families in their area just a short walk up from the beach on Post Road. Previously, the Schwartz family had resided near the Marine Air Terminal in Queens, where he was accustomed to falling asleep amid the noise and the lights of takeoffs and landings. Still, he enjoyed the lake; in the winter it was a frozen pond. And he had his few fellow sub-teen Waubeekan friends—including one of the Krate girls—who also attended Danbury's public schools. Occasionally, some summer friends came up on weekends and joined in.

Soon after their marriage, the Zwangs moved from Manhattan and took over Dave's parental home, which had been winterized due to the malfunction of an unreliable space heater. One summer morning, potentially toxic fumes that "backed up" chased Dave, his parents and two brothers out of their house and convinced them it was time to upgrade. For the young couple, the possibility of living rent-free was a great inducement to reside where he had enjoyed his summers as a young man. And they liked the "quiet and peacefulness" that came with being one of the two families on Alan Road and among "maybe a dozen [others] spread out" on the mountain, even if snow removal on some basically deserted streets was haphazard. Business opportunities would take Chris and Dave away from Waubeeka from 1973 to 1976, only to have them return for Dave to start his printing business

Waubeeka's frozen pond. *SNF.*

Unplowed Paul Street in wintertime. *AS.*

in town and to a different, permanent home. They came back in time to witness the shift in Waubeeka's demographics from a summer colony to a year-round neighborhood.

Some soft statistics indicate that the four-season population began to grow in the early 1980s. During that era, 40 percent of the houses—upgraded originals and new homes—were used more than "three to six months of the year." That number included folks who stayed at Waubeeka after Labor Day and the start of the New York City school year until the weather turned cold. Predominantly seniors—not the hardiest of souls—did not wish to cope with the snow, ice and cold temperatures that almost annually froze over the lake. The ice-skating and hockey that the young Schwartz and his friends enjoyed so much surely was not for them. "Snowbirds"— as they are euphemistically called—went off to Florida and other warm climes. If their neighbors were "neighborly," the year-rounders kept an eye on their houses. For those who remained, a sign of spring was "when the Florida license plates appear."

For Don and Sondra Rosenberg, who bought a house in 1979, the returnees ended the isolation that they coped with successfully for eighteen

This page and next: Winter sports on and off the frozen pond. *Courtesy of Chris Zwang, George Benitez, Neil Radisch and Dan Schwartz.*

years on Post Road. He recalled that "of the five houses, [they] were the only ones who lived there in the winter," although "some of [their] friends did come up on weekends." They ended their "loneliness" only when Don retired in 1998 and they relocated to Boynton Beach in Florida, returning to the lake for the summer.

The departures caused a collateral problem for the community. To help finance their months down south, some homeowners rented out their places to college students from Western Connecticut State University and from other local colleges who, to say the least, did not have the best interests of Waubeeka in mind. The worst among them trashed their rentals and broke into the unoccupied houses all around them in search of "booze and beds." Unintentionally, Sidney Klein did not help the law-and-order situation when, in 1985, he told the *News-Times* the community was "seasonal and the houses were empty much of the year." Immediately thereafter, a rash of burglaries afflicted the mountain.

In response, the community engaged a 24/7 guard service to stop the unwanted at the base of the Approach Hill. "The electronic gate was added later to address issues of cost and personnel working conditions deficiencies. The gate was moved up the hill in 2000." Security consciousness has, by and by, led to some embarrassing moments on the beach, like the time in the summer of 2012, when a new homeowner was confronted by "a militant woman [who] came up…and asked if [they] lived here. She was very serious and a bit scary." Fortunately, the confrontation ended quickly when the interrogator was told "we bought [a house on] Carol Street just five days previously and got a pass!" On the other hand, the presence of the gate and the commitment to tighter security have proven an attraction to singles, especially women who have bought homes and feel safe during the off-season. Jen Castello, who bought Harold and Ruth Pollack's home in the summer of 2020, was not fearful for herself but felt that the security spot "made her mother feel better." At the same time, other Waubeekans are not thrilled with the "aesthetics" of the gate, which evokes images either of a "penitentiary or an old-age home."

In 1982, the Zwangs were blessed with their first child. That meant by the end of the decade, decisions had to be made about schooling for Matt and later Carrie. Getting their son off the mountain was not a problem. They had a second car. And because enough school-age kids were now on the mountain—one estimate places, as of 1990, the community year-round percentage population at 75 percent—including weekenders, a parking area at the foot of the hill was constructed for drop offs and pick-ups.

Lake Waubeeka, a gated community. *SNF.*

In time, that carved-out space, abutting Starrs Plain Road, became a place where parents waiting for the afternoon bus got to know one another, sparking their own friendships. Such was the cordial experience of George and Amelia Benitez, a quiet, keep-to-themselves couple who bought on Marion Street right after their marriage in 2000. Soon after they settled, these devoted children of elderly parents convinced Amelia's parents to purchase a house on Paul Street, where they could keep tabs on them. In return, the grandparents were available to "day care" the Benitezes' three youngsters. When their older boy, Simon, was ready for school, George and Amelia found moms and dads of similar ages and responsibilities also milling around at the foot of the hill. Friendly conversations soon led the neighbors to dividing up the five-minute carpool chore. When it was their turn, the welcoming Benitezes were sure to offer after-school snacks to youngsters. Ultimately, the parents began socializing informally in their several homes.

Parent transportation ended when teenage children passed their road tests. Now these better behaved—but not always perfectly so—young Waubeekans could bring their friends into the community for "recreation and partying." To a great extent, another generation of young Waubeekans could feel that they were "campers without counselors," though if they drove too quickly around the narrow roads, adults yelled at them, "Slow down." Speed bumps were installed in the first decade of the new millennium.

Of greater weight to the Zwangs and other parents was the question of where the kids actually would go to school. For engaged Roman Catholic families—a subtle evidence that Waubeeka now had an increasingly religiously diversified population—St. Mary's School in Ridgefield offered a K-12 program for their children. A few committed Jews were attracted to the elementary school education that the Maimonides School in the Miry Brook section of Danbury proffered through grade 4. However, most families looked to public education for their kids. For some, the quality, size and culture of Danbury High School was a sticking point. The Zwangs believed that staying local was a point of emphasis. They wanted their children to experience a racially and ethnically "diverse" environment. Chris recalled, "Why would we take our kids out of reality where everyone is the same?"

Another family on their own street felt differently and opted for a school twenty-five minutes away in Wilton that reportedly possessed a superior academic reputation. Other families awaited their children finishing their secondary education in the New York area before fulfilling their long-term wish of full-time residence. It also made abundant sense for mothers and fathers who taught in schools beyond Danbury to take their youngsters with them on a daily basis.

In 2018, Tim and Lori Vickers faced the difficult question of whether to continue living on the mountain given their sons' educational progress and athletic abilities. Caden and Conor had both done well through fifth grade in a Danbury magnet school. They had "hit the lottery" for entering their boys into that top-notch grammar school program. But now middle school and ultimately high school were on the horizon. Also in play for this family was that the youngsters were budding, and hopefully, outstanding lacrosse players. Ridgefield's schools, in their view, had a somewhat superior academic and better sports program. While they were concerned with the lack of diversity in Ridgefield, as devout Christians—Tim has worked in Christian outreach work—they felt they would have "more of a community" in Ridgefield. Their lives revolved around school and church. But they still loved Waubeeka, which had been their home since 2004, and wanted to remain connected. So they rented their Paul Street house and, as homeowners, frequented its beaches, where they met up with their former neighbors.

While Waubeeka has remained on balance a majority nuclear family community, during the most recent decades, it has also been home in increasing numbers to couples—straight and gay—without children and single men and women. Julie Thompson, a local real estate agent who knows Waubeeka well, having worked with its houses since 2010, has identified, among year-rounders, not only families from Danbury who have discovered the affordable lake properties but also "single women from Ridgefield" and other sister areas as among the most anxious to buy into what she called "the neighborhood." These folks have looked "to downsize their home footprint," and the security system has been decidedly a large plus. The unexpected and frightening pandemic of 2020 caused a rush on properties in the spring of that horrible year as it did all over Fairfield County. By the summer of 2020, the stock of available houses was almost empty.

Meanwhile, Carol Nicklaus and Bruce Clark, self-described "official seniors of Alan Road," have been fixtures on that street since the 1990s. For years, they referred to themselves as the owners of the "Itkin House" after the name of the prior residents. They appreciate "the serene and secure location, activities, access to good neighbors, a sense of 'community.'" To date, the idea of relocating to a "senior living facility in the area" is not for them, though it has crossed Carol's mind that "establishing a real 'continuing care retirement facility' right here would be an excellent idea." Among a younger set, some men and women who grew up in Waubeeka with memories of many wonderful summers have returned to the lake as full-time residents. Though not constituting a chain migration, they have reignited friendships year round.

Arthur Brody grew up on the corner of High Street (now known as Sage Road). He now resides, with his partner Suanne Lowy-McManus, a few steps from Lesnick's Cove, that bend in the road on Carol Street where Max and Sue Lesnick—Waubeeka originals—used to live. In 1985, Brody fulfilled his long-held wish of living full time in Waubeeka when he and his wife, at that time, bought a home on Upper Carol Street not far from where he was raised. He has recalled that when he "woke up on Saturday morning, there was no [other] place I would want to be than in Waubeeka...an oasis in the woods." Though hardly antisocial, he liked the "cabin in the woods" feeling, the "quiet, isolation" at a time where—as noted—less than 40 percent of the lake was occupied through the winter. But commuting back and forth to work in Manhattan daily "burned" him out, particularly after Pete Couchevitz retired and his successor did not do as proficient a job in clearing the community's roads, not to mention the stretch on Starrs Plain Road to Route 7, which was

Connecticut's responsibility. The five-plus-hour round-trip trek back and forth from his high-pressure job in finance, where he sometimes worked late into the evening, was more than he could handle. His solution was to move to Katonah, New York, close to a Metro-North station, where he resided until 2011. For the next six years, he rented an apartment in New York City and came up to the lake on weekends. In 2018, he moved up full time, where he was able to work "from home two days a week." This advantageous schedule solved, in large part, his commuting issue. During the pandemic, he has worked "remotely."

Upon his return, he linked up with his erstwhile friends—some had kids, others did not—who had made their own moves back to the place they always had loved. However, group activities were circumscribed due to the cold weather. In the winter, the unheated main hall of the Community House was unavailable for large-scale events like the annual Coffee House and Art Show, which, in its several incarnations and venues, have been staples for generations during the summertime. In 2020, because of the pandemic, display of neighbors' visual and performing arts went virtual. That show had to go on!

Chris and Dave Zwang host their "extended family" of Waubeekans, past and present, circa 2010. *Courtesy of Dave Zwang.*

Art show and music on the peninsula, circa 1970. *Courtesy of Stanley Sinowitz and GC.*

Virtual coffeehouse and art show, 2020. *Courtesy of Debra Burger.*

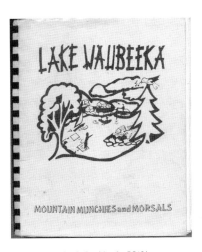

Cover of *LWA Cookbook. LWA.*

The after–Labor Day Halloween party was generally the last well-attended event on the community's calendar. In the months before spring, only eight or nine committed and warmly dressed yogis used the facility weekend mornings for their workouts, aided—by of all things—a space heater. Or they went downstairs to the small Sandy Brown Room, named for a young man tragically killed in a traffic accident. In prior years, the Brown Room was used as a hangout for teenagers. There has been some serious talk within the board over the last few years about the possibility of installing heat in the large hall. This expensive upgrade has yet to be approved. Accordingly, informal gatherings, "for dinner, [to celebrate] New Years or just to hang out" was the way year-round residents kept in touch. Sometimes they feasted on foods from recipes in the *LWA Cookbook*, produced during the off-season in 1980. In 2020, one of Brody's friends said that "we still get together," notwithstanding the pandemic "just in smaller groups, [we] don't want to tempt fate."

Others with no prior connections to Waubeeka also have found one another during wintertime. Bill Heese, who came to the community in 2003, remembered how the fires from cookouts and bonfires at the Paul Street Beach attracted neighbors who might have sledded down Cardiac Hill to join the party. Waubeekans with roots in Danbury frequent homes off the mountain, or their friends and relatives "come up," maintaining long-term relationships. Yuletide was an especially good time for family and friends of all backgrounds to come together in Waubeeka in the holiday spirit.

Halloween at the Community House. *LWA.*

Christmas at the Heese home. *Courtesy of Bill Heese.*

Then, there are others, young and particularly the old, who do not go to Florida and simply hibernate until the weather gets warmer. The Waubeeka archives are due largely to retiree Harold Pollack, who, with time on his hands and disdaining group activities, taught himself how to put community records in order. He and Ruth rarely left their house when it was cold outside. To keep themselves busy, Ruth read voraciously and played the piano, and Harold drew schematic diagrams of his water and electrical system. When Jen Castello bought her house in 2020, she would find these invaluable documents. They would be useful for modernizing that sixty-eight-year-old home.

On or about 2000, members of the synagogue group decided to get together when the weather was getting colder for services and communal meals on Thanksgiving weekend in November and Chanukah in December. But CMM's building was then unheated. One of the members, who owned a rather large house, opened her doors to her fellow worshippers. In an ironic twist of fate, this home on Post Road had been owned fifty years earlier by a family that was adamantly opposed to CMM. As of 2012, the synagogue's sanctuary and social hall—much smaller than and surely not competitive with the Community House—had a HVAC system.

6

CONCLUSION

Waubeekans Speak at the Beach

Waubeeka, and this volume, are both works in progress. But we have already discerned one essential, common thread that has united us over seventy years of history. We share an abiding love for our bucolic setting even if we have sometimes differed on the direction our lake "community" or, some say, our "neighborhood" should be taking. Ever a disputatious folk, even how we refer to our summer or year-round home or whether we have a "Community House" or a "Clubhouse" for our major indoor gatherings is itself an indicative point of linguistic contention that may differentiate old-timers from newcomers.

To gather a sense of where we go from here, a year ago, on Sunday, July 5, 2020, I put myself on "mute" and "zoomed' around the Paul Street beach with my trusty iPhone recorder in hand, and with Steven Frankel as our inquiring photographer, to hear what our neighbors appreciate about Waubeeka and what they look forward to see on our mountain in the years to come. Sadly, on that particular holiday weekend, due to the pandemic, there was no beach party. Still, scores of residents and friends turned out on a bright, sunny day. Even as most people adhered to social-distance decrees, varying groups of Waubeekans clustered together. They aggregated according to age, interests and long-term friendships. Parents and grandparents of the youngest sat close to the shallow water, keeping an eye on the non-swimmers in their family. Many of the oldest staked out room under the awning to limit exposure to the afternoon heat. They

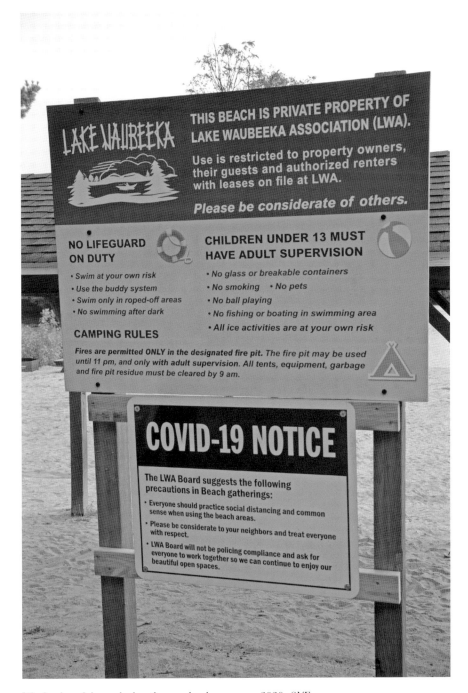

Waubeeka advisory during the pandemic, summer 2020. *SNF.*

searched for foursomes for bridge games. A younger crew took over a picnic table for their pinochle games. It has been Waubeeka's favorite card game from the days where some of their grandfathers played during down times in FDNY firehouses. One of the players admitted that his grandfather played this game better than he. Others took their places elsewhere in open spaces, baking in the sun or basking under their umbrellas. Then there were those who jumped into the lake, continuing their conversations while using a variety of flotation devices that once were strictly prohibited.

Intrepidly, Steven and I turned to each group and found a "representative" who spoke about where we are at this juncture and projected toward the future. After introducing ourselves and reassuring our neighbors that we had the best of motivations—we certainly were not the "Waubeeka Police," rudely inquiring whether they belonged on the beach—I conducted an "elevator interview." No one refused to answer my two-to-six-minute impromptu set of questions. Our interviewees reflected the varying types of backgrounds and experiences of those who had been more generously profiled earlier in the book. What they had to say underscores the patterns of behavior and attitudes that have been fundamental to Waubeeka's seventy-year history and perhaps for the future.

Bridge players on the Paul Street Beach, 2020. *SNF.*

Pinochle, Waubeeka's favorite game over different generations. *Courtesy of Pamela Gurock and LWA.*

The spokespeople included Glenn Colton, a third-generation Waubeekan who is the father of fourth-generation children; Gilson and Glaytia Silva, heads of a Brazilian American family, who bought a house only three months earlier; Russian American Lana Atanazevich, who has lived at Waubeeka for thirteen years with her husband, children and those whom she calls "her extended family" of cousins and closest of friends; Barbara Courtian, a proud grandmother, who has lived almost fifty summers at the lake; Jesse Uhrman, former president of the association; and finally Rachel Yehuda, who with her husband, Mitch Rothschild, was instrumental in the growth of CMM. This encore presentation of elements of our history may serve as a literary time capsule. It is an edited and interpretive version of our neighbors' thoughts, hopes and aspirations.

Colton is the ultimate Waubeeka "blue blood." Both sets of grandparents— Robert and Tessie Linn and Harry and Florence Colton—were original homeowners, and his parents, Alice and Ed Colton, now married over sixty years, were the first Waubeekans to marry each other. Thus, though not actuarially exact, Glenn feels that "I was here before I was born." But what is certain is that his connection to Waubeeka past, present and future is more than genealogical and historical. He has purchased and now lives in the Linns' former home. He remembers "the one for all spirit when I was

"The one for all spirit when I was young." Glenn Colton. *SNF.*

"A safe and secure community." The Silva family. *SNF.*

young" that was once the hallmark of the place. Of course, as a child, he did not attend those wild membership meetings.

The Silvas, understandably, after three months on the mountain, do not yet possess a strong sense of Waubeeka's story. But to hear Gilson and Glaytia talk, they sound like dyed-in-the-wool long-time residents. In time, they will find out what they like and what annoys them, maybe just like homeowners who date back to the 1950s. For them, among the community's attractions is its security. Their children can come home from school on their own, before Glaytia returns from work. Gilson, a painter who works in the surrounding towns and cities, can make it back home every night. Commuting is clearly not an issue for them. If Gilson has any complaints about the family's new community it is that his fellow Waubeekans don't always follow community rules. Perhaps, in time, he will speak up at a community meeting—much like those who came before him—albeit with calm and probity, about his unhappiness when he sees dogs unleashed on the road or at the beach or when his neighbors park where they are not permitted on Waubeeka's narrow roads.

Lana Atanazevich and her family did not find out about Waubeeka as part of a chain migration, from newspaper ads or from a real estate agent. Rather, idiosyncratically, with her husband working in Westport,

"Waubeeka is frozen in time." Lana Atanazevich. *SNF.*

Connecticut, and looking for a summer home, they took out a map of Connecticut, drew a radius of close traveling distances "to a lake" and happened on this community. As she peered out from behind the awning at her neighbors, at "families doing their thing" in and out of the water, she mused that "it was quite difficult to tell what year it was. [Waubeeka] is frozen in time." And not unlike a real old-timer, she hoped that what had always been "would stay that way."

Sitting among her fellow bridge enthusiasts, Barbara Courtian did not hear Lana Atanazevich's trope about a community "frozen in time." But in her own way, she shared that sensibility as she saw her granddaughter sunning herself with her friends mid-beach. When she and her late husband, Martin, first rented a house in 1969 and bought one two years later, they were welcomed into that circle of friends that had come together from Forest Park Crescent in Queens. The integration was seamless, and at least two of the group was still playing bridge fifty years later. What has pleased Courtian most is that "children of my friends became very good friends." And she "would like to see [her] grandchildren take over the house and have their friends become the best of friends."

Jesse Uhrman has seen it all during his seventy years at Waubeeka. And for fifteen years as a board member and as president from 2000 to 2005,

"The children of my friends became very good friends." Barbara Courtian. *SNF.*

he helped address all the issues that arose as the community completed its transition from a summer colony to a year-round neighborhood. Having lived the life of so many of the community's episodes, it is unsurprising that for him "what makes Waubeeka special is the way the community evolved about family, friends...neighbors who built the community together, starting from the ground up. It has changed over generations but for the most part the community has remained the same." But, for Uhrman, while continuity is worthy of hallowing, he hopes for "greater diversity; different cultures, different colors, different people" making up the future around the lake. His leadership style was "collaborative...to move our community forward into a more progressive future." Presently, he frequently is called upon to assist the next generation of leaders, particularly with his expertise toward ensuring that the lake remains as pristine as possible.

Similarly for Rachel Yehuda, as she looked ahead, a goal to strive for is the complicated task of "connecting to the past of Waubeeka's founding fathers and mothers through living out the dream that someone conceived of a long time ago" while building a "community where all will be accepted for whom they are."

Thus, looking toward the future, the challenge, as the 100 percent Waubeekan scion Glenn Colton suggested, is to have a diverse but unified

"Waubeeka has changed over generations, but for the most part the community has remained the same." Jesse Uhrman. *SNF.*

"Living out the dream that someone conceived of a long time ago." Rachel Yehuda. *SNF.*

community and not a "set of pods...old-timers, full-time residents, the religious community" each carving out their own places on the roads, Community House and at the beach. Hopefully, our ever-contentious neighbors will continue to fight over details—problems that at the moment seem all so important—while keeping in mind that we are all in Waubeeka together.

POSTSCRIPT

On Tuesday, August 4, 2020, the very day that the penultimate version of this book was completed, Hurricane Isaias smashed into Lake Waubeeka. Thankfully, no one was injured, but power lines were brought down and a number of houses were seriously damaged. The community was, however, blessed with a devoted maintenance crew that swung into action. And in true Waubeekan spirit, neighbors helped neighbors cope with the unexpected problem. One neighbor offered "the community the ability to charge their phones, laptops, iPhones, etc." Another used his chainsaw to clear the roads. A third volunteered to check on the status of

Victor and Carol Cohen's home in disrepair after Hurricane Isaias. *SNF*.

the homes of those who were not on the mountain. These were but some of the good deeds that were performed spontaneously from the Approach Hill to Carol Street and Post Road and every street in between. Reacting to the outpouring of concern that she saw all around her, newcomer Jen Castello was moved to comment: "I've only been here a little over a month but I'm so impressed with the sense of community up here....I am so truly happy to be here," even though a hole was blown in her roof. Her neighbor Joe climbed up to cover the gap. Castello's remark led long-time homeowner Carol Reher Cohen, whose house was hit hard by a fallen tree, to link the hurricane to the ongoing problems of the pandemic: "If it's this good during a pandemic. I can't wait to see it afterwards."

ABOUT THE AUTHOR

 Jeffrey S. Gurock is the Libby M. Klaperman professor of Jewish history at Yeshiva University. The son of first settlers at Lake Waubeeka, Gurock has spent seventy summers in the community. Jeff and his wife, Pamela, are proud of their three third-generation children and nine fourth-generation Waubeekan grandchildren.